# YOUR AMAZING BODY MENDS A
# BROKEN BONE

WRITTEN BY **VICKI COBB**   PHOTOMICROGRAPHS BY **DENNIS KUNKEL**
ILLUSTRATIONS BY **ANDREW N HARRIS**

**Lerner**

Lerner Books · London · New York · Minneapolis

NOTE: The photomicrographs in this book were taken with a scanning electron microscope (SEM). The photos are originally in black and white. A computer program is used to add colour, often to highlight interesting features. The colours used do not show the real colours of the subject. The × followed by a number indicates magnification. For example, ×250 means the object in the picture is 250 times larger than its real size.

For Jillian Davis Cobb  — VC

This series is dedicated to my mum, Carmen Kunkel, for the care she gives her children and grandchildren  — DK

For Jean, thank you for the experience and opportunities  — ANH

With special thanks to Dr Robert I, Cristofaro, Clinical Associate Professor of Orthopaedic Surgery, New York Medical College, Valhalla, NY, and Director of Paediatric Orthopaedic Surgery Westchester Medical Center, Valhalla, NY; Dr Sue Ott, Associate Professor of Medicine, University of Washington; and thanks also to Mary Slamin and Gail Fell, children's librarians from the Greenburgh, New York Public Library.

First published in the United Kingdom in 2009 by
Lerner Books,
Dalton House,
60 Windsor Avenue,
London SW19 2RR

Website address: www.lernerbooks.co.uk

This edition was updated and edited for UK publication by Discovery Books Ltd.,
First Floor, 2 College Street, Ludlow, Shropshire SY8 1AN

British Library Cataloguing in Publication Data

Cobb, Vicki.
Your amazing body mends a broken bone. -- 2nd ed.
1. Bones--Wounds and injuries--Juvenile literature.
2. Wound healing--Juvenile literature.
I. Title II. Cobb, Vicki. Your body battles a broken bone.
617.4'41044-dc22

ISBN-13: 978 0 7613 4423 0

Printed in Singapore

A broken bone happens quickly, and it's a nasty surprise. First, you feel a sharp pain. Then you feel a deep ache that doesn't go away. Your whole body reacts to the break. You might feel cold. You might feel dizzy and even pass out.

The good news is that you will recover. Different parts of your body work as a team to put your broken bone back together – with the help of a doctor, of course. Meet the superheroes of your own body. This book tells their story.

OSTEOBLAST

NEUTROPHIL

FIBROBLAST

BLOOD CELL

MACROPHAGE

STEM CELL

Your bones support your entire body. Without them, you would be a blob. Your muscles attach to your bones so that you can move. Like the rest of your body, your bones are alive. Your whole body is made of tiny living things called cells.

NERVE CELL

MUSCLE CELLS

BONE CELLS

RED BLOOD CELLS

Cells are so tiny that they can only be seen with a microscope – a very powerful magnifying glass. You have different kinds of cells for the many jobs in your body.

Inside your body, there are two kinds of bone. Compact bone, also known as cortical bone, is hard and very strong. It makes up the shafts of long bones. Under the microscope, we can see that compact bone is packed in layers around a tiny central hole. This hole is actually a hollow tube, or canal, that holds very small blood vessels and nerves. Blood flowing through these blood vessels brings food and oxygen to the bone cells, or osteocytes.

COMPACT BONE CROSS SECTION ×1075

BLOOD VESSELS

BONE MARROW CAVITY

OSTEOCYTES

Hard, bony material surrounds the osteocytes. Calcium is a mineral that makes compact bone hard. Calcium also makes our teeth hard. Our main source of calcium is from milk and cheese. Vitamin D, which our bodies make using sunshine, helps our blood keep up its calcium supply. Strong bones depend on both calcium and vitamin D. One of the jobs of the osteocytes is to maintain the calcium in bones, making sure they stay hard.

See what happens when calcium is removed from a bone. Put a clean chicken leg in a jar with enough vinegar to cover the bone. Let it sit for several days. Wash the bone. It's so rubbery that you can tie it in a knot!

If you break open a chicken bone, you can see the spongy bone inside. You can also see the red bone marrow.

COMPACT BONE

SPONGY BONE

BONE MARROW

The other kind of bone is spongy bone. It is like a honeycomb with lots of spaces. Spongy bone is found on the inside of compact bones. It is not as strong as compact bone, but it is much lighter.

The centre of the spongy bone is filled with blood-rich tissue called bone marrow. Bone marrow is the body's blood cell factory. Red blood cells, which carry oxygen to all parts of the body, and white blood cells, which fight diseases, are made in the red bone marrow.

# BONE MARROW CAVITY

×785

COMPACT BONE

BLOOD VESSELS

STEM CELLS

This is a slice through a bone showing the cavity filled with yellow bone marrow.

OSTEOCYTES

When you are about five years old, the marrow in the centre of long bones becomes yellow instead of red. The yellow colour is due to the fat stored there.

The yellow bone marrow can change back to red and make red blood cells if a lot of blood is lost. Some white blood cells are also formed in the yellow bone marrow.

The cells in the bone marrow that make the blood cells are stem cells. All new blood cells start out as stem cells. Stem cells are amazing because they can become many other kinds of cells. You'll find out more about them later in this story.

A broken bone, like any injury, damages cells so that they start dying. The injury breaks blood vessels and destroys muscle cells in and around the bone as well. The damaged bone cells give off a chemical that is a signal to the rest of the body that help is needed.

The liquid part of blood is straw coloured. Blood is red because it is full of tiny red blood cells. A drop of blood has about five million red blood cells in it. Blood also carries white blood cells. These are actually clear.

×3,655    **BLOOD VESSEL WITH RED BLOOD CELLS**

Blood immediately rushes to the rescue. Since a number of blood vessels are broken, some of the blood seeps into the area and causes swelling. In a few days, the blood may show through the skin as a colourful bruise.

If you think you've broken a bone, you should go to a doctor straight away for an X-ray. An X-ray is a kind of light you can't see. X-rays can travel through the soft tissues of your body, but not through your bones. After the X-rays pass through you, they record a picture onto photographic film. The places where the X-rays pass through your soft tissues and strike the film are dark. White areas are where the X-rays have been blocked, so your bones appear white. A doctor can clearly see if your bone is broken.

FRACTURES

Most broken bones are caused by a fall. The most common bone to break is in the wrist because it's natural to stick out your hand when you feel yourself falling. Your wrist takes the force of your landing as you try to stop a fall.

The X-ray tells the doctor if the bone needs to be moved into position or if pins have to be put in to hold it in place. Don't worry. If your break needs this kind of treatment, you'll be given some medicine so you won't feel any pain.

**X-RAY OF PINS AND STAPLES IN A BROKEN ANKLE**

This is an X-ray of a foot after its broken bones have been repaired with metal pins and staples in an operation. The foot is now healed and as good as new.

The one thing your bone needs to heal is rest. This means that you should not move it, even a tiny bit. That's why the bandage for a broken bone is a stiff cast that holds the break in a fixed position. Make friends with that cast. You're going to be wearing it for at least a month, possibly two.

Some broken bones can't be put in a cast. A broken collarbone, rib or toe will heal by itself. Pain when you move warns you to keep the bone still while it heals.

While you're getting an X-ray and a cast, your body is working alongside the doctor to help you heal. Large numbers of a kind of white blood cell, called a neutrophil, move onto the scene. Neutrophils remove the dead bone and muscle cells from the injury site. They also give off juices that are signals to other cells that help is needed. As the healing continues, the neutrophils are joined by similar cells called macrophages.

Neutrophils and similar cells called macrophages change shape by forming bulges on either side of a dead cell or germ. The bulges grow longer until they meet around the dead cell, which is then inside the neutrophil. Once inside, the neutrophil 'digests' the dead cell. It continues this job until it too dies. Later, macrophages come in to clean up any remaining debris, including dead neutrophils.

×13,885    NEUTROPHILS

Other helpful cells in the blood are fibroblasts. They make thread-like structures that create a loose mesh through the injured area. The fibroblasts form a kind of scaffolding that lays out the plans for new bone to fill in. Small blood vessels start growing around and through the mesh, bringing blood and other cells to help repair the damage.

It's about three days after the injury, and the mop-up is almost complete. Some more of your body's superhero cells are getting ready to spring into action and repair the fracture.

Stem cells can become many other kinds of cells. They turn into the kinds of cells that build new bone at the break. Building new bone is complicated. Stem cells are the real heroes of the healing process.

STEM CELLS

×9,960

Stem cells are truly amazing! Many scientists are doing research on them because of their ability to change into all kinds of different cells. Here's how they do it. A stem cell splits into two parts. One part remains a stem cell, and the other becomes the new, needed cell. This new cell can reproduce others like itself. Healing a fracture is one natural way your body uses stem cells, but doctors and scientists are working on ways to use stem cells to cure other medical problems.

Stem cells go to each end of the fracture. Some of them
become bone-making cells, called osteoblasts. Other stem cells go to the
inside of the fractured bone to become cartilage-making cells, called
chondroblasts. Cartilage is a flexible material, like soft plastic. You find it
at the end of long bones (knees, ankles, elbows, shoulders and wrists)
and the tip of your nose. Cartilage is often later replaced by bone,
especially in children's bones as they grow. The same thing happens
with a break — the cartilage in a broken bone is temporary and will
be replaced later by bone.

# FRACTURED COMPACT BONE ×785

OSTEOCYTES

The triangular shape surface along the top of the photomicrograph shows the smooth outside surface of a compact bone. The bumpy part is the fracture, which has exposed the osteocytes.

The osteoblasts produce a growing network of fibres at both ends of the break. The chondroblasts keep making cartilage in the inside of the bone. The new bone and the new cartilage areas keep getting larger until they meet. This new material around the fracture is called callus. Callus gives back some of the strength to the broken bone. But it is not healed yet.

Blood carries minerals to the woven bone and cartilage to make them stronger. About two weeks after the fracture, new cell workers, the osteoclasts, show up. The callus of woven bone and cartilage is disorganized compared to your original bone, which was formed in beautiful tiny layers.

So the osteoclasts dissolve the quickly made callus. The osteoblasts start laying down new bone. After a month or two, the fracture is strong enough that the cast can come off. But *still* the healing isn't finished.

The doctor will remove your cast with a saw. Your skin will be pale with a whitish coating on it. Your skin is always shedding dead skin cells, and normally they just fall off. But the cast prevents this from happening, so the coating of dead skin cells piles up. A good scrubbing in the bath or shower should solve the problem.

**×240** DEAD SKIN CELLS

The yellow layer on the left is made up of flattened, dead skin cells that your body constantly sheds. They are replaced by the red layer of living cells.

Your arm or leg will also look skinnier than your unbroken limb. When you don't use your muscles, they shrink. Since you've been in a cast, you've lost some muscle. But a few weeks of using your muscles again will make them come back to normal.

The bone cells need to feel the pull and push of your muscles. Activity helps the bone cells to make sure the bone is just the right size and shape to support your muscles. Your body actually remembers the shape and design of your original bone.

About three months after a fracture, your healed bone is as good as new. Doctors have discovered that you must use your bones to keep them healthy. So celebrate your healed bone by running, skipping and jumping. The more you exercise your bones, the stronger they become.

# GLOSSARY

**blood vessels:** tubes that carry blood

**bone marrow:** the soft tissue found in the hollow insides of bones. Red blood cells are produced here.

**calcium:** an element that is absorbed by the body and makes bones hard

**callus:** a temporary structure of fibroblasts and chondroblasts that forms around a broken bone at the beginning of the healing process

**cartilage:** a flexible connective tissue that is found at the ends of long bones, in the nose and in the outer ear

**cells:** the smallest units of all living things considered to be alive. The smallest living things have only one cell. Humans are multicelled.

**chondroblasts:** cells that make cartilage

**compact bone:** hard, dense bone that makes up most of the outside layers of bones of the body. It is packed with calcium.

**fibroblasts:** cells that form connective tissue fibres. They are especially important in repairing a wound.

**fracture:** a crack or break in a bone

**macrophage:** a white blood cell that cleans up sick and infected areas by 'eating' germs and dead cells

**minerals:** compounds in nature with definite chemical formulas

**osteoblasts:** cells that make new bone cells

**osteoclasts:** cells that dissolve bone cells by reabsorbing the calcium. They are essential for reshaping a bone as it heals from a fracture.

**osteocytes:** star-shaped cells trapped deep inside compact bones that help maintain the minerals in compact bone. They are originally osteoblasts.

**photomicrograph:** a photograph taken with the help of a microscope

**red blood cells:** the cells in the blood that carry oxygen to all parts of the body. Their red colour comes from iron in each cell.

**spongy bone:** a layer of honeycomb-like bone lining the hollow insides of long bones surrounding the marrow cavity

**stem cells:** immature cells that are capable of making many other types of cells

**white blood cells:** colourless cells floating in the blood that help the body fight disease

**X-ray:** a photograph that doctors use to see how a bone has been fractured

# FURTHER READING

Ballard, Carol. *The Skeleton and Muscles* (Exploring The Human Body) Franklin Watts, 2005.

Claybourne, Anna. *Complete Book of the Human Body* (Internet Linked) Usborne Publishing Ltd, 2006.

*Eye Wonder: Human Body* Dorling Kindersley, 2006.

Parker, Steve. *Muscles and Skeleton* (Our Bodies) Wayland, 2006.

Treays, Rebecca and Christyan Fox. *Understanding Your Muscles and Bones* (Internet-Linked) Usborne Publishing Ltd, 2006.

Walker, Richard. *The Human Skeleton* (Body Science) Franklin Watts, 2004.

# WEBSITES

**KidsHealth**
http://www.kidshealth.org/kid/exercise/safety/broken_bones.html
This site offers details on various kinds of bone fractures.

**Kids First for Health**
www.childrenfirst.nhs.uk/kids/health/ask_doc/body_bits/childrens_bones.html
This site has loads of information about the structure of bones, broken bones and ways to protect your bones and keep them healthy.

# INDEX

First published in the United States of America in 2009
Text copyright © 2009 by Vicki Cobb
Photomicrographs © 2009 by Dennis Kunkel
Illustrations copyright © 2009 by Lerner Publishing Group, Inc.

Additional photographs in this book are reproduced with the permission of: © Edward Kinsman/Photo Researchers, Inc., pp 14, 16; © Eye of Science/Photo Researchers, Inc., p 27.